Small Faith

By Keith Hodges

Small Faith - Keith Hodges

Table of Content

Chapter 1

The Shift 5

Chapter 2

Enough Faith.......................13

Chapter 3

The Key.............................19

Chapter 4

The Impossible Is Possible........32

Chapter 5

Change The Equation.............48

Chapter 6

Just Like Jesus.....................54

Connect with Pastor Keith

Facebook @keithhodges.798

libertychurchcampuses.com

Chapter 1
The Shift

This book is an extension of a message I preached at our Church. If you had been in the service that day, you would have received a small individual pack of mustard. Maybe you have one lying around your house, or perhaps the next time you go through a drive-through and get mustard for your sausage biscuit, you will remember the message of this book. I pray that mustard will become a visible reminder of one of the greatest truths in scripture. Are you ready for it? Ok, here it is. You already have everything you need to live the life God has called you to live. Because you don't need big faith, you just need small faith in a BIG God.

> You already have everything you need to live the life God has called you to live. Because you don't need big faith, you just need small faith in a BIG God.

This book is going to help you to make the shift. A shift in our thinking moves us from disqualified to qualified because small faith qualifies us to live the life God has for us.

So this book is really about a shift in our thinking. It's about shifting the way we think about faith. And the biblical word for changing your thinking is repentance. When you repent, you change the way you think. As we work through this book, we will talk about a specific shift in the area of faith. We are going to change the way we think about our faith in Christ. We will recognize some significant lies we have believed regarding faith and having enough faith to receive your miracle. To receive your breakthrough, to receive the things God has purposed, planned, and already promised in his word, through his Son, Jesus Christ. So we're going to shift our thinking. And what's going to happen is this shift will move us from a place of being disqualified where I can't receive; to be qualified to receive every good and every perfect thing God has for us.

Shift Your Thinking

I don't know if you've ever bought a house, but there's this strenuous part when you're going through the loan process where you're getting qualified for the loan, and everybody's wondering, well, how much am I going to be qualified to borrow? Probably more than you want to pay back. But here's the realization, there is something powerful about being qualified because the moment you get qualified for that loan, you can walk in confidence that you can buy the house of your dreams.

Once you know, you've been qualified for a hundred thousand, two hundred thousand, or five hundred thousand, whatever it might be in your situation. The moment you're qualified, you begin to walk in confidence that says, anything in my price range, I can purchase. Well, I'm going to give you some excellent news today. You have been qualified by faith to receive everything God has for you. Stop and consider what I'm saying; Faith allows you to receive everything God has for you. Small faith is about us shifting our thinking to a place where we begin to recognize I am qualified, and if I'm qualified, I can walk in confidence.

And if I'm qualified, I can walk in boldness. And if I'm qualified, then I can step into every situation in every circumstance in my life, knowing that not only do I have enough, but I've got more than enough to meet the demands and the needs that are going to come against me.

And I can receive every good thing God has promised for my life. Are you ready for that? Matthew 17:14-19 says, "And when they had come to the multitude, a man came to him, speaking of Jesus, kneeling before him and saying, Lord have mercy on my son, for he is an epileptic and suffer severely for his often falls into the fire and often into the water. So I brought him to your disciples, but they could not cure him. But Jesus answered and said, Oh, faithless and perverse generation. How long shall I be with you? How long shall I bear with you? Bring him here to me. And Jesus rebuked the demon, and it came out of him; the child was cured from that very hour. And then the disciples came to Jesus privately and said, Why could we not cast it out?"

Let me be honest with you. I've had some private conversations with the Lord. That sounded like the disciples, Why did I pray and nothing happened? Lord, why am I believing, declaring, and speaking the life you've called me to live, and I do not see any results, I know your word promises? Have you ever had any of those conversations? Lord, why couldn't we cure him? Why couldn't we deliver them? Why couldn't we set them free?

> Have you ever had any of those conversations? Lord, why couldn't we cure him? Why couldn't we deliver them? Why couldn't we set them free?

I know I've preached some funerals; I should have never preached. I've gone to the hospital knowing

God wanted to heal but walked away with death sentences. Things did not change, but I know in my heart they were supposed to. I know the same works that Jesus did I should be doing. That is the commission of the gospel; Christianity is not about just getting through life successfully. Christianity is not just about you dying and going to heaven. Christianity is not about obtaining a measure of success where you live a comfortable life, and you don't have to worry about the bills or the mortgage. No, Christianity is about you walking at a level of faith where you begin to do what Jesus did and live like Jesus lived and do greater works than he did because he has gone to the Father. Christianity is about what we're going to unpack on each page of this book because small faith is the secret to living that kind of life.

Look at the next verse because I love how Jesus answered this question. Why could we not cast it out? Jesus said, because of your unbelief, for I tell you if you have faith as a mustard seed, listen to what he is saying. If you have faith as a mustard seed, you will say to this mountain, Move from here to there, and it will move, and nothing will be impossible for you.

Notice what he didn't say; he didn't say nothing will be impossible for God. He said nothing would be impossible for you.

If you have faith, small faith, mustard seed faith, then you can say to any mountain, be thou removed and cast into the sea and it will obey you, and nothing will be impossible for you.

Jesus didn't say we needed big faith. He didn't say we needed more faith. He just simply said we needed small faith. Mustard seed faith was enough to move the mountain, and nothing would be impossible to us. Why couldn't we heal him? Why couldn't we do what Jesus did?

The problem wasn't they needed more faith. Jesus said the problem was you didn't have any faith. He said all you need is small faith. Now, let me tell you the lie we have believed. The lie we have believed in the local Church is simply this; I need more faith.

> The lie we have believed in the local church is simply this:
> I need more faith.

Have you ever said or have you ever heard somebody say if I just had more faith? If I just had more faith, the breakthrough would have come. If I just had more faith, the provision would have come. If I just had more faith, they would have been healed. If I just had more confidence, things would have turned out different. All those statements are lies based on a scheme of the enemy.

Jesus did not say they needed more faith; Jesus said they needed small faith. You just need a mustard seed of faith. Mustard seed is the smallest seed you can imagine. Jesus said that's all you need. You don't need big faith. You don't need more faith. You just need mustard seed faith. You need small faith. And here's the lie and scheme. We have moved from a place of faith in God to where we have faith in faith.

When you say I need more faith, you're saying that you have faith in your faith. It is the size of your faith that gives you confidence instead of the size of your God. Jesus told the disciples, have faith in God, isn't that what he said? Have faith in God.

Hebrews 11:6 says, "they that come to God must believe that he is because without faith, it's impossible to please God, and he is a rewarder of those who seek him."

We have to come to God by faith. It is small faith in a big God that changes the circumstances, the mountains, and the impossibilities in our lives.

I love to hear people preach and teach on faith. But one of the challenges of faith teaching is if you don't take faith teaching back to its source, which is not faith in faith. It's faith in God. We somehow start to believe we need more faith and a bigger faith and greater faith. If I just had more faith, I could do the things God has called me to do. No, no, no, no. Let's change our thinking.

Let's repent. Let's shift the way we think. We don't need more faith or immense faith. We just need small faith in a BIG God.

Let's repent. Let's shift the way we think. We don't need more faith or immense faith. We just need small faith in a BIG God.

Chapter 2
Enough Faith

God has already, please read these words carefully; God has already given us enough faith to move every mountain in our lives, and the proof is in salvation.

If we have enough faith to be saved, then we have enough faith. Stop and think about that for a second.

If we have enough faith to be saved, then we have enough faith. If you are reading this book and you've been born again, you already have enough faith.

> If we have enough faith to be saved,
> then we have enough faith.

Would you agree with me today that the greatest miracle that can ever happen in a person's life is the miracle of salvation and transformation that occurs when someone is born again? The greatest miracle is the miracle of salvation. Every other miracle pales in comparison. Have you ever considered what happens when a person gets born again? You go from being destined to a devil's hell to an eternity in heaven with God. You go from being in bondage to freedom. You go from being dead in sin and a slave to sin to becoming a son or a daughter of the most high God. The Bible says God translates you from the kingdom of darkness into the kingdom of God.

You go from being blind where you can't see to having eyes where you can see. Your ears are open, where you can hear the voice of God; your heart is made alive.

Think about it. All of this happens when you get born again. Every other miracle pales compared to the salvation and transformation from being born again because every other miracle is temporal. The miracle of salvation is eternal.

I mean, when you get born again, you get to spend forever and ever and ever and ever and ever and ever in heaven. If you get healed of cancer, you're still going to die. You get raised from the dead; you're still going to die. You have a leg grow back; an arm grows back, you're still going to die. But if you get born again, you'll never die.

So here's the revelation, if you have enough faith to get saved, then you have enough faith to experience the greatest miracle. Then how dare we say we don't have enough faith to experience temporal miracles? Small faith is all we need because you already have enough faith to move every mountain. And the proof is your salvation. The fact that you're here today and you're not who you used to be is a miracle.

I've been transformed. I've been delivered. I've been set free. I've been made whole. The power of God has changed me. I'm not who I used to be, how about you. And if you've got enough faith to experience salvation, you've got enough faith to move every mountain in your life.

Listen to what the Bible says, Ephesians 2:8 (NKJV) "For by grace, you have been saved through faith and that not of yourselves. It is a gift of God."

Galatians 3:26 (NLT)" For you are all children of God through faith in Christ."

Romans 5:1 (NLT) "Therefore, since we have been made right in God's sight by faith, we have peace with God because of what Jesus Christ our Lord has done for us."

2 Peter 3:9 (NKJV) "The Lord is not slack concerning His promise, as some count slackness, but is long-suffering toward us, not willing that any should perish but that all should come to repentance."

Let me rephrase that last verse; it's not God's will that any should perish, but that all people should come to salvation.

John 3:16 (NKJV) "for God so loved the world that he gave his only begotten son that whosoever would believe in him would not perish."

Titus 2:11 (NKJV) "For the grace of God that brings salvation has appeared to all men."

John 3:17 (NKJV) "For God did not send his Son into the world to condemn the world, but that the world through him might be saved."

I know you have enough faith to move every mountain. I know you have enough faith to receive every good thing God has for you because God is not willing, the Bible says, for anyone to perish. So think about; if it is God's will for everybody to be saved. Even though we understand not everybody is right with God, people reject the saving grace of Jesus Christ. What a tragedy that people would turn their back on the gift of God through his Son, Jesus Christ. Everybody is not saved, but we understand it is the will or desire of God for all people to be saved. So if God desires you to be saved, then God has to give you the faith to experience salvation.

So look what Romans 12:3 (NKJV) says "For I say, through the grace given to me, to everyone who is among you, not to think [of himself] more highly than he ought to think, but to think soberly, as God has dealt to each one a measure of faith."

> God gave you a measure of faith so that every person on planet Earth has enough faith to accept the saving grace of Jesus.

It is the will of God that every man is saved. And guess what? For you to accept salvation, the Bible says there's only one way to be saved, you are saved by grace through faith in Jesus Christ. We've become sons and daughters of God through faith in Jesus Christ. We are justified in the eyes of God through faith in Jesus Christ. So guess what God did. God sent His son to pay the penalty, the price for your salvation. God gave you a measure of faith so that every person on planet Earth has enough faith to accept the saving grace of Jesus Christ.

God has given every man, every woman, every person enough faith, the measure of faith, to believe in, the gift of God, to believe in the grace of God, to believe in the sacrifice of God's Son.

And if God has given you enough faith to believe and be saved, then you have enough faith to move every mountain, to receive every miracle, and to walk in all that God has for you because the proof of your faith is in your salvation.

The devil's lied to you. You know, you're saved, but you don't believe you have enough faith to be healed. You've received salvation, but you don't think you have enough faith to prosper. You've received salvation, but you don't believe you have enough faith to get free of the thing that's been holding you back. But if you have been born again, you have enough faith.

You can begin to walk in the supernatural God has for you because you don't need more faith. You need small faith, and you already have enough faith. You should be shouting right now! You've got enough faith, and guess what, if you haven't been born again, God has given you a measure of faith, and you can receive the most incredible miracle known to humanity; eternal life. Just ask God right now to save you, confess your sin, confess Jesus as your Lord and Savior, you can be born again. Welcome to the family!

Welcome to the family!

Chapter 3
The Key

So small faith is the key that opens every door and moves every mountain. When you read the Bible, you will find out everything you receive in the kingdom of God comes by faith. Salvation, healing, deliverance, and prosperity comes by faith. Everything you receive in the Kingdom of God comes by faith. The Kingdom of God is a kingdom of faith.

All we have to do, I want you to hear this. All we have to do is believe. Let me repeat it one more time; all we have to do is believe.

Do you remember when you got saved? Do you remember where you were when you got saved? You heard the gospel of salvation, you came under conviction, and you realized you were a sinner, and Jesus was the savior. There was no hope apart from him. And you believed if by faith you would trust in him, he would save you, forgive you, and give you eternal life in a place called heaven. A place you've never seen or been to, but you believed it. And when you believed it, you probably did something crazy like pray a prayer.

I mean, I love salvation prayers. I've seen people get saved, delivered, and set free from a lifetime of sin, addiction, and strongholds by praying this real powerful prayer. God, if you're real, help me. How simple is that; God, if you are real, help me, and at that moment, their lives forever changed. A simple prayer prayed with small faith.

Everything in the kingdom of God comes by small faith; all you have to do is believe. Now, let's qualify that statement; you operate in faith when your behavior matches your belief. I'm going to say that again; when your behavior matches your belief, you're operating in faith. Why is that important? It's important because you can go through religious rituals without having faith in your heart toward God.

You can have faith in faith. You can have faith in people. But it's when you put your faith only in God that something happens. It's when you place your faith in God, miracles happen. It's when you put your faith in God, souls are saved, and lives are changed. When you put your faith in God, the supernatural becomes natural, and the impossible becomes possible.

> You can have faith in faith. You can have faith in people. But it's when you put your faith in God that something happens.

So it's not just about behavior; we have to believe. Have you ever heard the old saying, let's just fake it till we make it? And I understand that I understand some elements you just press through, and you keep doing the right thing until the right thing begins to happen. And I'm good with that concept in the proper context. On my job, in my family, with my finances, I have to keep doing the right thing no matter how I feel or what I might even believe.

The challenge with that thinking is we think it's the behavior that will produce belief or faith. If I just keep doing the right thing, then one day, I will believe. But behavior without belief won't create lasting fruit.

But if I believe and I allow my belief to dictate my behavior. It releases faith. When I let what I believe dictate my behavior, faith comes. So I know I'm in faith when what I believe and how I behave come together? So it's not a belief with no action, and it's not a behavior with no faith. It's the combination of the two. Look what the Bible says.

James 2:21-22 (NLT) 21 "Don't you remember that our ancestor Abraham was shown to be right with God by his actions when he offered his son Isaac on the altar? 22 You see, his faith and his actions worked together. His actions made his faith complete."

His faith and his works came together when what he believed and how he behaved match. All of a sudden, it released faith. And it was faith that was made complete by the combination of those two things.

Let's look at Mark 5:25-34 (NLT) 25 "A woman in the crowd had suffered for twelve years with constant bleeding. 26 She had suffered a great deal from many doctors, and over the years, she had spent everything she had to pay them, but she had gotten no better. She had gotten worse. 27 She had heard about Jesus, so she came up behind him through the crowd and touched his robe. 28 For she thought to herself, "If I can just touch his robe, I will be healed." 29 Immediately, the bleeding stopped, and she could feel in her body that she had been healed of her terrible condition. 30 Jesus realized at once that healing power had gone out from him, so he turned around in the crowd and asked, "Who touched my robe?" 31 His disciples said to him, "Look at this crowd pressing around you. How can you ask, 'Who touched me?'" 32 But he kept on looking around to see who had done it. 33 Then the frightened woman, trembling at the realization of what had happened to her, came and fell to her knees in front of him and told him what she had done. 34 And he said to her, "Daughter, your faith has made you well. Go in peace. Your suffering is over."

Small Faith - Keith Hodges

This is one of my favorite stories in the Bible. The Bible says a woman in the crowd had suffered for 12 years with constant bleeding. She had suffered a great deal from many doctors. And over the years, she had spent everything she had to pay them, but she had not gotten better. She had gotten worse. I love this story because here's a picture of what I believe is true for many of us. Physically, financially and relationally, you have done everything you know to do. And instead of getting better, you got worse.

Physically, you're doing all the right things. Financially you're doing all the right things. You're pouring out all this money; you're investing time. You're pouring out all this effort, and the world says, we'll just try a little harder.

> Physically, financially and relationally, you have done everything you know to do. And instead of getting better, you got worse.

And even the Church says, just keep trying. Try a little harder. You need to read your Bible a little bit more. Pray just a little bit longer, and everything will work out.

I want to tell you something. You can read your Bible and pray until you can't read your Bible and pray anymore, and until you have faith, nothing happens. But when you believe, small faith, not big faith, not more faith, just a mustard seed of faith. The same faith you used to get saved is the same faith you use to receive every good thing God has for you; you are qualified.

Just like when you qualify for that loan, you can look at that two hundred thousand dollar home, and you know, you are qualified. You can walk into the house and walk through it like you're going to own it one day because it's your house. And when you are in faith, guess what you can do. You recognize your small faith has qualified you to receive everything God has for you. You can read the Bible and the Bible says all the promises of God are yes, in Christ Jesus.

2 Corinthians 1:20 (NKJV) "For all the promises of God in Him are Yes, and in Him Amen, to the glory of God through us."

You can read about his healing and deliverance, salvation, and provision, and you can say that is mine. You can stop reading and take a praise break; small faith qualities you to receive everything God has for YOU!

The scripture said she had done all she knew to do, and then she heard about Jesus. Consider that phrase; she heard about Jesus. The Bible says faith comes by hearing and hearing by the word of God. Let me tell you why it's essential that you go to a church that preaches the whole Council of God. "Because faith comes by hearing and hearing by the word of God." Romans 10:17

And if you're not in a church that's preaching healing, deliverance, breakthrough, salvation, transformation, provision, and prosperity. If you are not in a church that says everything that Jesus did, you can do (John 14:12), then you are in the wrong Church.

Because faith comes by hearing and hearing the word of God, I've met people who went to Church for 20 years and, after 20 years of faithfully going to Church, finally got saved in another Church. Because they never heard they needed to be born again.

> "Faith comes by hearing and hearing by the word of God." Romans 10:17

People have told me, I went to Church for 20 years, and I never felt conviction and never heard the truth of the scripture that says, "You must be born again." (John 3:7) Then they go to another church one Sunday; they hear the gospel, faith then comes by hearing, and all of a sudden, after 20 years, they had faith to be saved.

This woman in scripture had suffered for twelve years, then she heard, Jesus heals. She heard, Jesus delivers. She heard Jesus could change everything that was happening in her life. She heard, and she came up behind him through the crowd and touched his robe; look at verse twenty-four. She thought to herself, here's her faith.

If I can just touch his robe, I will be healed. I don't need Jesus to stop and give me a word. I don't need him to call my name out of the entire audience. She said all I have to do is just touch the hem of his garment. If I can just touch him, I will be healed. So she heard, and she believed. When her belief matched her behavior, guess what happened. Verse twenty-nine, says "immediately the bleeding stopped."

She felt immediately she had been healed of this terrible condition. I want to tell you something. I'm so glad we serve an immediate God. I understand sometimes there's a process, and I know sanctification is a process of becoming more and more like Jesus. I know all that, but I'm so glad we serve the God of the immediately, the God of the suddenly. Instantly healed, and suddenly you can be delivered.

God can do in a moment what you could never do in a lifetime because he is a supernatural God. Small faith changes everything.

> God can do in a moment what you could never do in a lifetime because he is a supernatural God.

Immediately she was healed, and she felt it. I love she could feel in her body that she had been healed. We serve a God you can feel. You can feel His presence; you can feel His power because He is REAL.

Verse thirty tells us, Jesus realized at once that healing power had gone out from him, so he turned around to the crowd and asked who touched me? And his disciples said, Lord, look at this crowd pressing around you. How can you ask who touched me? But he kept on looking around to see who it was. Then the woman, trembling, realized what happened to her, came and fell on her knees in front of him and told him what she had done. And he said, daughter, Your faith has made you well, go in peace. Your suffering is over.

Your suffering is over. Today is the day of salvation. Now is the appointed hour. This is your day. Come on, this is your day, for your miracle, healing, deliverance, for your suffering to be over because small faith in a big God changes everything.

Before we move on from this story, I want you to see one last point; small faith is the difference between touching Jesus and receiving from Jesus everything you need. Everybody was touching Jesus, but only one person received from him. When Jesus said, who touched me, the disciples looked at him, said, Jesus, are you crazy?

Everybody's touching you, Jesus; you're the superstar, the celebrity, and the main attraction. Everybody's touching you. Everybody's grabbing you. Everybody wants your autograph. Everybody is after you. I mean, we got selfies going everywhere with Jesus.

But Jesus said, no, no, no. Someone touched me with faith; small faith made the difference. Small faith placed a demand on the power of God that was available to all but only accessible to those with faith.

There is a difference between just going through the religious motion and believing God is who he says he is. You can read the Bible, pray, go to Church and touch Jesus all day long. You can brush his hair, you can straighten this robe, you can wash his feet, but until you have faith. You won't receive what he has for you. Remember, faith is the key that unlocks everything in the kingdom of God.

Here's the good news, you've got enough faith, you're qualified, small faith qualifies you to receive what God has for you. Everybody was touching Jesus, but small faith helped her receive healing from Jesus.

I told you I love this story. I love this story because it removes the barriers of religion, big faith, and all the crazy ideas surrounding the supernatural. Here is the moral of the story, we don't need a particular word from God; we just need small faith. This lady with no name got healed without Jesus's permission. Think about it; she got healed without his consent. When she touched him with small faith, the power went out of his body, and Jesus said, Who touched me?

He didn't know who it was. He didn't know what had happened. The disciples of Jesus said everybody's touching you, but the Bible says he kept looking. Do you know why? Because he didn't know what had happened. All he knew was the power of God had gone out of him. All he knew was a miracle had taken place. All he knew was somebody with faith reached out and touched the hem of his garment, and it placed a demand on the power of God in his body, and it went out of him without his permission.

We need faith—small faith in a big God who loves us.

So you don't need a special word from God. He's already spoken. Unfortunately, what was happened is we get these things confused in our minds. We think, If I go to Church tomorrow and the Pastor calls me out of the crowd by name, then I know I'm going to get healed. We think, if a red bird lands on my windowsill, flaps its right-wing three times, flies around the house, lands on the other windowsill, flaps his left-wing three times, then I know I will be delivered. We work up these ideas in our minds because we want our miracle, but we need faith— small faith in a big God who loves us.

You don't need a word from God. He's already spoken. You don't need his permission to get what he's already qualified you for. Did you hear that? You don't need his permission to get what he's already qualified you for. When the bank qualifies you for two hundred thousand dollars, you don't call them every time you walk in a two hundred thousand dollar house and say, I just want to make sure I can buy this house. The banker says I qualified you three months ago. Buy the house.

All you need is small faith in a big God, and the good news is, you already have faith. God has already given you the measure of faith. You're already qualified. You're pre-approved for everything God has for you. Small faith gives you access to all he has; faith is the key that unlocks every door.

Chapter 4
The Impossible Is Possible

The next step in our spiritual shift comes in the area of our thinking regarding the impossible. When you read the Bible, you will recognize God does the impossible, and people in the Bible also performed some pretty impossible things. This creates a challenge for most of us because you probably feel pretty ordinary like me. So please read the following statement slowly, and let's consider what it means.

God never asks us to do the impossible. But he does ask us to believe the impossible is possible.

We will look at Hebrews chapter 11, and we're going to work through what is called the hall of fame of faith. In Hebrews 11, the Bible recounts many of the Old Testament's miracles, signs, and wonders. Amazing things God did through ordinary people. What we're going to see is God never asked one person in Hebrews 11 to do the impossible. He just asked them to believe the impossible was possible, small faith. Many Christians believe that God could never use them in supernatural ways to do what Jesus did because I just don't have enough faith. We have to eradicate this lie. We have to shift the way we think because most have already disqualified ourselves from the impossible.

We think I can't do that. I can't heal that person. I can't save anyone, and I can't do what Jesus did. God is not asking you to heal or save anyone, but he asks you to pray healing over them. God is asking you to share the gospel with them so they can get saved. God isn't asking you to walk on water, but He asks you to get out of the boat. God never asked you to do the impossible. He only asked you to believe, to believe with mustard seed faith the impossible is possible.

> God never asks us to do the impossible. But he does ask us to believe the impossible is possible.

Hebrews 11:1 says, "Now faith is the substance of things hoped for and the evidence of things not seen."

Hear what the scripture says; faith expects the good. That's what hope is. Hope is an expectation of good, and faith expects the good God has promised. Faith is the substance of things hoped for. The world tells us all the time, don't get our hopes up. But God says, if you don't get your hopes up, nothing's going to change. There has to be an expectation of faith. So faith releases hope. My small faith in a BIG God releases an expectation of hope. How do you know you're in faith? You know you are in faith when you expect good things to happen. Think about that for just a second. Faith expects good; faith looks at every day with an expectation of good. Because God is good, I believe good things will happen to me and flow through me.

Let's flip the coin, because unfortunately, we identify with the opposite side a little more. How do you know when you're in fear? You know you are living in fear when you expect bad things to happen.

When you think, no matter how hard I try, I'll never get ahead. You are always waiting on the next shoe to drop. When something good happens, you automatically begin to wonder what is going to go wrong. So, you know, you're in fear because you expect bad things to happen. You know, you're in faith when you expect the goodness of God. David said in Psalms 23, surely goodness and mercy shall follow me all the days of my life. Surely goodness and mercy shall follow me all the days of my life because God anoints me. God leads me and provides for me. God favors me. God loves me. God surrounds me. He lives in me. God goes before me and stands behind me. And good, good, good, good, good things are going to happen in my life. Because that's what faith does, faith releases an expectation for good, and you begin to expect good things in every area of your life.

Hebrews 11:1 says, "Now faith is the substance of things hoped for and the evidence of things not seen."

Small Faith in a BIG God releases spiritual vision. Faith is the evidence of things not seen; faith sees what God says as a reality. When you see what God says is a reality in your life, it is done. When you see the marriage restored, you see your body healed. You see yourself walking in prosperity and blessing; you see your children restored. You see salvation in your household. You see favor on your job. When you see it, you're in faith. You have spiritual eyes that see what God says, and you see it as a reality.

Occasionally people will ask me, did you ever imagine Liberty Church was going to be this big? It almost sounds arrogant to tell them the truth because the truth is, I see Liberty Church being massive. When we started Liberty Church with three couples in a storefront building, I saw North Alabama's Greatest Church, saw a church shaking the nations for the glory of God, saving souls, making disciples, destroying the works of the devil. We are just getting started; we have just touched the tip of the iceberg.

Faith sees what God says as a reality. Early on, I had somebody tell me, Pastor Keith, you really shouldn't say that because it sounds arrogant. But I am not arrogant; I am an advocate for the local Church. I believe God has a plan and a purpose for every Church, every Pastor, and every believer. But I also know what God said to me when we opened the doors of Liberty Church on July 5th, 1998. I believe what God says is a reality. Small faith in a BIG God sees what God says as a reality.

Small faith in a BIG God sees what God says as a reality.

Hebrews 11:6 (NKJV) "But without faith [it is] impossible to please Him, for he who comes to God must believe that He is, and that He is a rewarder of those who diligently seek Him." Nothing is impossible with faith, but without faith, it's impossible to please God. Faith makes the impossible possible because faith connects us to God.

One of the ways you know you are walking in faith is faith connects you to God. Faith draws near to Him; small faith in a BIG God keeps you connected. Faith creates resilience. When life knocks you down, faith not only gets up but keeps coming back to God. Remember, it is not faith in faith or faith in yourself but faith in God that makes the impossible possible. The moment you stop drawing near to God is the moment you stop walking in faith. Now let's look at the next verse.

Hebrews 11:7 (NKJV) "By faith, Noah, being divinely warned of things not yet seen, moved with godly fear, prepared an ark for the saving of his household, by which he condemned the world and became heir of the righteousness which is according to faith."

Recognize something; what Noah did was not impossible. Noah was not the first guy to build a boat. Noah will not be the last guy to build a boat. God never asked Noah to do the impossible. He asked him to build a boat; yes, it was a massive boat. But it wasn't impossible, was it hard? Yes, it was hard; it took him a hundred years. But it wasn't impossible; it was possible. God said Noah, build a boat, and then once Noah had done His part, God did the impossible. God provided the animals; God sent the rain, God flooded the Earth. What did Noah do? Noah built a boat, and he built it by faith, believing in what God said. He expected that something was coming. His faith made him persist. Do you think after one year he was tired, after five years, after 80 years of building this boat? But it still wasn't done. Finally, one hundred years later, his faith became a reality. God never asks us to do the impossible, but he does ask us to believe the impossible is possible. Faith persists; faith is the only thing that could keep one person working on one task for one hundred years.

As I'm writing this book, I am over twenty-three years into the process of building "North Alabama's Greatest Church." I can't stop because God's not done. I'm still building, doing the possible, believing God for the impossible. Small faith is powerful because it creates persistence.

Noah prepared the ark for the saving of his household. Let this encourage you; you can create a safe place for your family to grow up. It's not impossible to have the passwords and the codes to every social media account your child has. It's not impossible to look at their phone regularly and see who they're talking to and what they're talking about. It's not impossible to walk in the room now and then, raise the mattress to see if there's something under it. Is it hard work? Yes. Is it seemingly unending work, yes? Is it impossible, NO? Is your family worth it, YES they are!

Too many times, we give up, make excuses, and lay down on the job. But if you believe God has a purpose and a plan for your family, specifically your kids, then it's worth it. Small faith goes a long way in creating persistence to keep doing the possible, knowing God will do the impossible.

> Too many times, we give up, make excuses, and lay down on the job.

Marriage, parenting, paying the bills, and juggling a career may be challenging, but it's not impossible. If by faith you'll do the possible, God will do the impossible. He will revive, restore and rebuild broken hearts, dreams and careers. Small faith makes the impossible possible because it connects us to a BIG GOD! Now let's look at another element of faith.

Hebrews 11:8 (NKJV) "By faith, Abraham obeyed when he was called to go out to the place which he would receive as an inheritance. And he went out, not knowing where he was going."

By faith, Abraham obeyed; faith produces obedience. God didn't ask Abraham to do the impossible; he just asked him to obey. Pack your bags and go, but God, I don't know where I'm going, but God, I've never done this before. Faith obeys not knowing the end result but knowing the one who is calling you to go.

Has God ever asked you to do anything impossible? He's asked you to pray, give, serve. He's asked you to get up early, stay up late, go out of your way to help someone. He's asked you to love people and care for them. He's never asked you to do anything impossible. By faith, Abraham obeyed, God provided the place, God provided the inheritance, God provided the provision, God provided everything they needed. God will also provide for you. You know you are in faith when you obey the simple prompting of the Lord. You know you are living by faith when you live with a "yes Lord" on your heart. We disqualify ourselves because we think we could never do the great things we see others do, but the truth is. We don't have to do great things, we just have to obey, and God will do the rest.

Hebrews 11:11 (NKJV) "By faith Sarah herself also received strength to conceive seed, and she bore a child when she was past the age, because she judged Him faithful who had promised."

> Faith conceives when our bodies won't.

By faith, Sarah received the strength to have a child. She was barren, and she was past the age of having children. Sarah could not have a child. But Sarah could believe God. Sarah couldn't get pregnant; she had tried her entire married life.

But she could believe God would give her a baby. This verse is powerful because this situation is so challenging. Kellie and I have walked with many couples over the years who wanted a baby and could not get pregnant. They did everything they could do. They had all the treatments and went to all the doctors. It's heartbreaking and overwhelming. If you are in that situation right now, my heart and prayers go out to you. Let me encourage you with the scripture. By faith, Sarah received the strength to conceive. You don't have to get pregnant. You just have to believe God wants to give you your heart's desire. Faith conceives when our bodies won't.

Mark 11:23-24 (NKJV) 23 "For assuredly, I say to you, whoever says to this mountain, 'Be removed and be cast into the sea,' and does not doubt in his heart, but believes that those things he says will be done, he will have whatever he says. 24 "Therefore I say to you, whatever things you ask when you pray, believe that you receive [them,] and you will have them."

Sarah couldn't get pregnant, but she could believe it. Faith focuses us on what we can do, not what we can't do. Faith believes and speaks those things our heart desires. You can believe in your heart and speak with your mouth; faith decrees what it believes.

Hebrews 11:21 (NKJV) "By faith, Jacob, when he was dying, blessed each of the sons of Joseph and worshiped, [leaning] on the top of his staff."

Small faith in a BIG God releases blessings. Jacob blessed his children and grandchildren. When's the last time you blessed your children and declared that they would be a mighty nation for the glory of God? When's the last time you blessed your children and told them they were going to shake a nation for the glory of God, that they were called, anointed, blessed, highly favored, and God was going to use them to change a generation for the glory of God? When's the last time you blessed your children with that kind of blessing? Jacob blessed them in faith because he was dying. He knew physically and financially he was not going to be there to help them. Jacob wasn't going to be able to do anything in the natural. So guess what he did? He believed, he believed that God wanted to prosper his children. He believed his grandchildren were going to be mighty for God. As for me and my house, we will serve the Lord. How about you? When you have faith, you bless.

You bless your job; you bless your family; you blessed your car. You bless your career; you bless your finances. When you have fear, you curse. When you're afraid, you curse. The people that curse their lives are people who are afraid of living them. I used to curse money. I would curse it because I didn't know how to handle it; I was afraid we wouldn't have enough money. I was worried we weren't going to be able to pay the bills. So I would say, I hate money, I wish we didn't have to have money, I wish I could live without money. Each of those statements was curses; I was speaking. Fear causes you to curse; you'll curse your job, your curse your family, your curse your children, your curse yourself. When you're afraid, you'll begin to curse your own body. The doctor gives you a diagnosis, and if you allow fear to take over, you'll start cursing your body. Well, the doctor said, I'm not going to live; the doctor says I'm not going to make it through the year. The doctor says my health will decline; the doctor says nothing's ever going to change. I praise God for doctors, but doctors aren't God. They don't have the final authority over your life. The doctor diagnoses the problem, tells me what I am fighting, and identifies my enemy, but he doesn't define my victory. Small faith in a BIG God declares the blessing; I'm delivered and redeemed. I'm getting stronger and stronger, better and better. My latter years are going to be better than my former years.

I praise God for doctors, but doctors aren't God.

Fear curses and faith blesses. You know you're in faith when you bless, and you know, you're in fear when you curse. If your adult children are not serving God, it's easy to allow fear to curse your children by saying they're never going to change. They're never going to figure it out. No matter how much we pray, nothing ever happens. STOP cursing your family; God loves you and your children; believe that He desires your children to know him and serve him. Small faith blesses.

Hebrews 11:23 (NKJV) "By faith Moses, when he was born, was hidden three months by his parents because they saw [he was] a beautiful child, and they were not afraid of the king's command."

By faith, Moses's parents hid him, and they resisted the command of a crazy king because they believed Moses was special. They believed he was chosen. They believed he had a purpose and a plan birthed in him by God. This is why you can't give up on your kids. This is why you can't kill them when they're teenagers (LOL). They are unique, chosen, and anointed. I love the scripture, which says God will pour out his Spirit on all flesh, and your sons and your daughters will prophesy. I pray that regularly over my children. God, I thank you, my children, will prophesy. My sons and my daughters will prophesy. Your world will be like fire, shut up in their bones in the name of Jesus. They will speak your word, and mountains will fall, and demons will tremble. The sick will be healed, and lost people will be saved. Why? Because I believe they are unique and I think you are special too. What do you believe?

Every person is fearfully and wonderfully made in the image of God. I believe God created you to declare His glory. I think every life matters, every soul is eternal, and every person was created by God and for God. Moses's parents believed it, and when they couldn't hide him any longer. They put him in a little ark, set him out on the river, and trusted God to do what they couldn't do. Think about how awesome God is. The guy (Pharaoh) who ordered Moses's execution would be the one who provided for Moses's raising. Pharaoh's daughter raised the deliverer that would break the back of Egyptian oppression and lead the children of Israel into the promised land. WOW, small faith in a BIG God changed everything. Moses's parents didn't do the impossible; they believed the impossible was possible.

Hebrews 11:29 (NKJV) "By faith they passed through the Red Sea as by dry land, whereas the Egyptians, attempting to do so, were drowned."

He believed God would do what he couldn't do.

45

Now Moses leads the children of Israel out of Egypt, and God leads them to the Red Sea. Pharaoh's army is behind them, and the sea is in front of them. The people begin to grumble in fear, but Moses heard from God. Stretch out your rod, the same rod he had used as a shepherd, the same rod he had handled a thousand times. God wasn't asking Moses to do the impossible; he had stretched out his rod many times. However, this time was different. There was an expectation, small faith in a BIG God. He believed God would do what he couldn't do. I'm going to do the possible, and God's going to do the impossible. I'm going to do what I can do, and God's going to do what I can't do. Then when he stuck out his rod, God sent the wind to divide the Red Sea, which the nation of Israel just walked through. And if you read that story, it is incredible because when the Egyptians followed them, the water consumed them and destroyed them. So in a matter of days, God destroyed the mightiest army on the planet. He delivered the Israelites from 400 years of bondage because of small faith in a BIG God. When we do the possible, God will do the impossible. A lack of faith does not disqualify us because small faith is enough.

You don't have to do the impossible. You just have to believe God can you do the impossible. Small faith moves mountains, and nothing is impossible to you because nothing is impossible with God.

Small Faith - Keith Hodges

Mark 11:23-24 (NKJV) 23 "For assuredly, I say to you, whoever says to this mountain, 'Be removed and be cast into the sea,' and does not doubt in his heart, but believes that those things he says will be done, he will have whatever he says. 24 "Therefore I say to you, whatever things you ask when you pray, believe that you receive [them,] and you will have them."

I want to ask you, what's your heart's desire? What is it? Picture it in your mind. Because God said that whatever you desire when you pray, believe you've received. All it takes is a mustard seed of faith for you to believe God can do what you can't do. Small faith is enough; you don't need more faith.

Small faith in a BIG God qualifies you to receive everything He has for you. Choose faith, choose to believe!

Chapter 5
Change The Equation

Small faith removes you from the equation and places the weight upon God.

For all you math geeks out there, you know equations are the keys to unlocking the mysteries of math. Small faith is powerful because it changes the equation. Usually, we look at the promises of God through the filter of our abilities, we don't believe the impossible is possible. Our natural way of equating life is based upon our abilities. We assume something is impossible if we don't have the resources, power, or ability to make it happen. Small faith looks at the promises of God through the filter of God's sufficiency, not our capabilities. We disqualify ourselves based on our abilities instead of being qualified based on His sufficiency. Let's look at Mark 11 again and bring in another truth from Romans.

Mark 11:20-24 (NKJV) "20 Now in the morning, as they passed by, they saw the fig tree dried up from the roots. 21 And Peter, remembering, said to Him, "Rabbi, look! The fig tree which You cursed has withered away." 22 So Jesus answered and said to them, "Have faith in God. 23 "For assuredly, I say to you, whoever says to this mountain, 'Be removed and be cast into the sea,' and does not doubt in his heart, but believes that those things he says will be done, he will have whatever he says. 24 "Therefore I say to you, whatever things you ask when you pray, believe that you receive [them,] and you will have them.."

> Small faith removes you from the equation and places the weight upon God.

Romans 10:17 "So then faith comes by hearing and hearing by the word of God."

These verses show us where faith comes from; the origin of faith is hearing. When we hear the word of God, it releases faith into our hearts. Then Jesus taught us faith is released by speaking. He spoke to the fig tree; he then told the disciples they could have what they say. Faith comes by hearing and is released by speaking. When you say what God says, you release faith. You hear, believe, speak and receive.

I can't count the times I have tried to get people to confess the word over their lives, and they resist. They resist because they say, I can't say that because it's not true. God's word is truth. Jesus said his word was spirit and truth. The truth is people won't say God's word because they don't believe God's word. They have believed the lie that their circumstances or feelings are more accurate than God's word. This thinking is ill-logical. We all know circumstances change, feelings change; what you thought was horrible has become a great thing. Your emotions and events lied to you; they told you life was over. But your life wasn't over; it was just beginning. God's word, on the other hand, never changes. Let's examine the virgin birth of Jesus and what Mary did to become the mother of God.

Luke 1:26-38 (NKJV) "26 Now in the sixth month, the angel Gabriel was sent by God to a city of Galilee named Nazareth, 27 to a virgin betrothed to a man whose name was Joseph, of the house of David. The virgin's name was Mary. 28 And having come in, the angel said to her, "Rejoice, highly favored one, the Lord is with you; blessed are you among women!" 29 But when she saw him, she was troubled at his saying and considered what manner of greeting this was. 30 Then the angel said to her, "Do not be afraid, Mary, for you, have found favor with God. 31 "And behold, you will conceive in your womb and bring forth a Son, and shall call His name JESUS. 32 "He will be great and will be called the Son of the Highest, and the Lord God will give Him the throne of His father, David. 33 "And He will reign over the house of Jacob forever, and of His kingdom, there will be no end." 34 Then Mary said to the angel, "How can this be since I do not know a man?" 35

And the angel answered and said to her, "The Holy Spirit will come upon you, and the power of the Highest will overshadow you; therefore, also, that Holy One who is to be born will be called the Son of God. 36 "Now indeed, Elizabeth your relative has also conceived a son in her old age; and this is now the sixth month for her who was called barren. 37 "For with God nothing (spoken) will be impossible."

> With God, nothing spoken will be impossible.

I have to stop right here. This literal Greek translation of verse 37 says; nothing spoken will be impossible. Wow, with God, nothing spoken will be impossible. Your small faith-filled word contains the power of the impossible.

God honors the spoken word when that word agrees with Him. Now let's look at the last verse in this reading.

Luke 1:38 "Then Mary said, "Behold the maidservant of the Lord! Let it be to me according to your word." And the angel departed from her."

Recognize, Mary didn't do the impossible; she believed the impossible. Small faith agrees with God. All Mary had was a word from God, but all Mary needed was a word from God. All you need is a word from God. Mary didn't impregnate herself; with small faith, she agreed with God and said, "be it unto me according to your word."

Psalms 107:19-20 (NKJV) "19 Then they cried out to the LORD in their trouble, And He saved them out of their distresses. 20 He sent His word and healed them, And delivered them from their destructions."

Listen to what this scripture says; they cried out to the Lord in their trouble, and He saved them. But the next verse tells us how he saved them. He sent His word, just like with Mary, God gives you a word when you have a need. Why, because without faith, nothing is possible, but with faith, all things are possible. God gives us a word; that's his part. We have to believe/agree with that word that's our part. When we believe what He says, God does what we can't do. Small faith in a BIG God moves mountains.

If Jesus supernaturally showed up in your room today and spoke a word of healing, do you believe you would be healed? If he spoke a word of deliverance, would you be delivered? If he said a word of financial blessing, would you be blessed? Guess what; he has already spoken a word over you. All the promises of God in Christ Jesus are yes and amen.

2 Corinthians 1:20 (NKJV) "For all the promises of God in Him are Yes, and in Him Amen, to the glory of God through us."

This one verse opens up the floodgates of heaven and allows us to drink from the well. Nothing is impossible for you because nothing is impossible with God. This verse implies that our yes to his promises invokes an amen from the Father to do what he promised he would do through His Son, Jesus. Faith pleases God because it honors the Father and releases His blessing into our lives.

---

2 Corinthians 1:20 (NKJV) "For all the promises of God in Him are Yes, and in Him Amen, to the glory of God through us."

Chapter 6
Just Like Jesus

We can do the same works and even greater works than Jesus because Jesus never did the impossible; he believed in the impossible.

Now before you stone me, consider Jesus's ministry. He never did the impossible. The impossible happened; the dead were raised to life, sick people were healed, and the blind could see. If you stop and think about what Jesus actually did, he was a vehicle for the impossible, but he never did the impossible. Jesus was entirely God, but he operated as a man; because he set the example for us to follow. If he did what he did as God, then I am disqualified because I am not God. But if he did what he did as a man filled with the Holy Spirit, walking in faith, then we can do what he did. The Bible records 37 miracles of Jesus, and we know he did many more because John 21:25 says "And there are also many other things that Jesus did, which if they were written one by one, I suppose that even the world itself could not contain the books that would be written. Amen."

Let's read some of the miracles of Jesus. Because everything that Jesus did, you can do, he didn't do the impossible - HE BELIEVED THE IMPOSSIBLE!

Matthew 9:28-30 (NKJV) "28 And when He had come into the house, the blind men came to Him. And Jesus said to them, "Do you believe that I am able to do this?" They said to Him, "Yes, Lord." 29 Then He touched their eyes, saying, "According to your faith, let it be to you." 30 And their eyes were opened."

What did Jesus do? He touched his eyes and said, according to your faith, let it be. You can do that. You can lay your hands on people and pray for them. You can be the vessel the power of God flows through.

Mark 3:1-5 (NLT) "1 Jesus went into the synagogue again and noticed a man with a deformed hand. 2 Since it was the Sabbath, Jesus' enemies watched him closely. If he healed the man's hand, they planned to accuse him of working on the Sabbath. 3 Jesus said to the man with the deformed hand, "Come and stand in front of everyone." 4 Then he turned to his critics and asked, "Does the law permit good deeds on the Sabbath, or is it a day for doing evil? Is this a day to save life or to destroy it?" But they wouldn't answer him. 5 He looked around at them angrily and was deeply saddened by their hard hearts. Then he said to the man, "Hold out your hand." So the man held out his hand, and it was restored!"

What did Jesus do? He said, hold out your hand; you can do that. You can encourage people to step out in faith. You can help people put their faith into action.

John 11:39-44 (NKJV) "39 Jesus said, "Take away the stone." Martha, the sister of him who was dead, said to Him, "Lord, by this time there is a stench, for he has been [dead] four days." 40 Jesus said to her, "Did I not say to you that if you would believe, you would see the glory of God?" 41 Then they took away the stone [from the place] where the dead man was lying. And Jesus lifted up [His] eyes and said, "Father, I thank You that You have heard Me. 42 "And I know that You always hear Me, but because of the people who are standing by I said [this,] that they may believe that You sent Me." 43 Now when He had said these things, He cried with a loud voice, "Lazarus, come forth!" 44 And he who had died came out bound hand and foot with grave-clothes, and his face was wrapped with a cloth. Jesus said to them, "Loose him, and let him go."

What did Jesus do? He said Lazarus come forth; you can do that. You can speak life where there is death.

> You can speak life where there is death.
> You can speak peace during your storm.

You can look at dead things; marriages, relationships, business, ministries and call them back to life.

Mark 4:39-40 (NKJV) "39 Then He arose and rebuked the wind and said to the sea, "Peace, be still!" And the wind ceased, and there was a great calm. 40 But He said to them, "Why are you so fearful? How [is it] that you have no faith?"

What did Jesus do? He said, peace be still, you can do that. You can speak peace during your storm. You can look at the chaos and speak peace. You can stop the argument with words of peace.

Matthew 14:15-20 (NLT) "15 That evening, the disciples came to him and said, "This is a remote place, and it's already getting late. Send the crowds away so they can go to the villages and buy food for themselves." 16 But Jesus said, "That isn't necessary--you feed them." 17 "But we have only five loaves of bread and two fish!" they answered. 18 "Bring them here," he said. 19 Then, he told the people to sit down on the grass. Jesus took the five loaves and two fish, looked up toward heaven, and blessed them. Then, breaking the loaves into pieces, he gave the bread to the disciples, who distributed it to the people. 20 They all ate as much as they wanted, and afterward, the disciples picked up twelve baskets of leftovers."

What did Jesus do? He blessed the food and gave it to his disciples; you can do that if you had disciples, LOL. You can bless the people and things in your life. You can bless your family, job, and health. You can speak blessings over everyone and everything in your life.

John 9:6-7 (NLT) "6 Then he spits on the ground, made mud with the saliva, and spread the mud over the blind man's eyes. 7 He told him, "Go wash yourself in the pool of Siloam" (Siloam means "sent"). So the man went and washed and came back seeing!"

What did Jesus do? He spits on the ground, made mud, and said, go and wash; you can do that. Ok, this one is kind of gross, but you can create a point of contact for other people's faith. You can challenge them to believe and act upon their faith.

So let's consider what Jesus did; he touched, spoke, prayed, and spits on the ground. We can do everything he did because he never did the impossible; he believed in the impossible. Let's allow this truth to settle upon our hearts. The Bible tells us the same Spirit that raised Jesus from the dead lives inside us. We don't have to do the impossible; the Holy Spirit inside us can do anything. He just needs a vehicle to work through. Our small faith allows the supernatural power of God within us to flow through us and do the impossible.

Small faith says you can have whatever you say, and you can do whatever Jesus did because nothing is impossible to those who believe. So, what do you believe? Let's refuse to allow fear, our lack of abilities, or insecurities to disqualify us. We are qualified; small faith in a BIG God is more than enough.

John 14:12 (NLT) "I tell you the truth, anyone who believes in me will do the same works I have done, and even greater works, because I am going to be with the Father.

As we close this book, my prayer is that your faith is stirred up. You are qualified; small faith is enough; you only need to believe, and the fruit of faith will flow through you, and God will do what you can't do. So grab you a mustard packet, put it somewhere you will see it every day, and remember; all you need is small faith the size of a mustard seed.

> We are qualified; small faith in a BIG God is more than enough.

Small Faith - Keith Hodges

Made in the USA
Columbia, SC
26 September 2021